Beyond the Millennium

Beyond the Millennium

by John Bird

Queenship
PUBLISHING COMPANY
P.O. Box 42028 Santa Barbara, CA 93140-2028
(800) 647-9882 • (805) 957-4893 • Fax: (805) 957-1631

"Happy is the man who reads this prophetic message, and happy are those who read it and heed what is written in it, for the appointed time is near."
— The Book of Revelation 1:3

"Write on a scroll what you now see and send it to the seven churches."
— The Book of Revelation 1:11

© 1998 Queenship Publishing

Library of Congress #: 97-75827

Published by:
  Queenship Publishing
  P.O. Box 42028
  Santa Barbara, CA 93140-2028
  (800) 647-9882 • (805) 957-4893
  Fax: (805) 957-1631

Printed in the United States of America

ISBN: 1-57918-052-3

Contents

The Lady of All Peoples 1

Church Notification 17

Beyond the Millennium 21

The Lady of All Peoples

The official notification from the Bishop of Haarlem, Monsignor Hendrik Bomers, on May 31, 1996, relates to the prayer and title "The Lady of All Peoples." The Bishop has officially given approval of veneration to Our Blessed Lady under the title "The Lady of All Peoples" and re-affirmed the Imprimatur given by his predecessor to the prayer in which this title was first included.

Monsignor Bomers is a very courageous and brave Bishop, working in a country where the true Faith and the teaching of the Catholic Church has been almost entirely extinguished. He has been inspired to give permission for the veneration of "The Lady of All Peoples" to proceed without impediment and in so doing has authenticated that the prayer received through the visionary Ida Peerdeman, contains nothing contrary to Catholic Faith or morals and that the title "The Lady of All Peoples" is an appropriate one especially in these times. The Church has not made any judgement on the messages and prophecies received through the visionary, and leaves it open to each individual to embrace or not.

Sadly, Ida Peerdeman died on June 17, 1996 at the age of ninety. She heard the news and the Bishop's notification fifteen days before her death. For fifty years she had remained faithful and strong in her faith and in the messages given to her despite very little support and encouragement from those in the Church to whom she looked for support. At the end of such a long "Way of the Cross" surely the good news she heard prior to her death would have given her tremendous joy. The Bishop, who attended her funeral, was glowing in his appreciation of her life's work and dedication, her humility and unswerving faith. Our Divine Lord tells us that His mother is the Mother of All Peoples, "Woman, behold thy son."

First Appearance in 1945

Our Blessed Lady first appeared to Ida in Amsterdam, on the Feast of the Annunciation, March 25th in 1945, exactly six hundred years after a Eucharistic Miracle there in 1345.

The apparitions in both Holland and Germany were to last from 1945 to 1959. In that time, She gave over sixty messages to the visionary, including many prophecies about future events. These messages can be divided into two parts, the first period from March 1945 to November 16th, 1950, and from then on to 1959.

In the first period She gave twenty-three messages in which She reveals why She has chosen to appear in these times and She prophesies events which would happen in the Church and in the world and warned us about the moral decline in all the nations of the world, and in the Church, which, if continued, would lead to catastrophe. In the second period from 1950 to 1959, Her messages emphasize certain theological truths which are taught by the Church, and She proclaimed a new Dogma — the last Dogma in Marian History.

Beyond the Millennium

From the messages, it is evident that She did not come just to predict future events, but as these have happened through the years, it is a clear sign and proof of Her apparitions. In fact, She said that She would give no signs except those in Her words. By this is meant that when an event is prophesied and takes place, we can take it as a sign of proof of the apparition. Her main purpose in Amsterdam was to reveal God's plan for mankind and to teach us how to invoke and seek the coming of the Holy Spirit of Peace into the world.

Our Lady does not focus on Herself, She focuses on the Redeemer and the Cross, in the shadow of which She stands. She affirms that Her messages are not only for one country, but for all peoples and all nations and should be spread as widely as possible and be read attentively. *"I am coming to talk to the whole world,"* She says and all Her messages, wherever they are given, are equally important and we could say that every apparition is, of course, linked to every other apparition. Again, She repeats that what She has said is for all peoples and all nations.

Dogma of Our Lady's Assumption

On November 1st, in 1950, Pope Pius XII proclaimed the Dogma of Our Lady's Assumption, body and soul, into Heaven. On November 16th, of that year in Amsterdam, She came and proclaimed a new title for Herself, "The Lady of All Peoples" - "The Lady of All Nations." She explained that this was linked to the last Dogma in Marian History, which had to come after the Dogma of the Assumption and which proclaims Her Co-Redemptrix, Mediatrix and Advocate. This Dogma is linked to Her title "The Lady of All Peoples" which will be conferred on Her on May 31st (She didn't say which year) and it will be Her crowning glory in Heaven.

Our Lady Stands in Front of the Cross

I am standing in front of the Cross as Co-Redemptrix and Advocate. Much conflict will arise about this Dogma, but the outcome has already been fixed in Heaven.

Beyond the Millennium

Never before in the Church has Mary *officially* been called Co-Redemptrix, Mediatrix or Advocate, but they form together a unity and this will be the keystone of Marian History and become the new Dogma. Because Mary is Co-Redemptrix, She is also Mediatrix and Advocate. Not only because She is the Mother of the Lord Jesus Christ, but because She is the Immaculate Conception.

This Dogma will be and is the crowning glory of your mother and when it is proclaimed the Lady of All Peoples will obtain peace, true peace for the whole world. I have come to tell this depraved and degenerated world — unite, all of you unite.

I will lead all the dispersed flock back into one fold. The Holy Spirit of Peace is nearer now than ever before, but He will only come if you pray. He has been in readiness since the beginning. He is the salt, He is the water, He is the light, He is the power that overshadowed your Mother. He has pro-

ceeded from the Father and the Son and it is He who has endowed the Lady of All Peoples with His power and because of this She can and may distribute grace to you.

Her new title is meant not only as a name of honor, but first and foremost as a program so that "The Lady of All Peoples" can be made known all over the world. The title and the dogma were only revealed on November 16th, 1950, because the Dogma of the Assumption had to come first. All other dogmas had to lead up to "The Lady of All Peoples."

The course of the Christian year is marked out by liturgical feasts all of which commemorate events of the past with the exception of one which celebrates in advance an event of the future. This feast is the Epiphany.

Both Christmas and the Epiphany commemorate the coming of Christ into the world; Christmas in respect to men individually — salvation is offered to everyone, and the Epiphany in respect to all the peoples of the

Beyond the Millennium

earth, all nations, so that they can acknowledge the Kingship of Christ.

The times in which we live, the Age of Mary, is a time when we join the Three Wise Men on the journey towards Christ, King of the Epiphany, and like them we are guided by a star, none other than Our Blessed Lady Herself. She is with us to lead all the nations of the world to the dawn of the Epiphany which lies beyond the darkness of the apostasy which now covers the whole of the earth.

Along the way, the star has stopped at many different places in the journey, at the Rue du Bac, La Salette, Lourdes, Pontmain, Fatima and recently in nearly every country and continent of the world. These are the mile posts to lead us to the anticipated Eucharistic Reign of Jesus, but it was in Amsterdam, more than in any other place, that the message of unity in the Church and of all the nations of the world, was proclaimed more directly than at any other stage of the journey.

Universal Unity

In Paris, in 1830, Our Lady revealed Herself standing erect on the globe of the world which was surrounded in clouds, Her hands outstretched streaming with rays of light. At Amsterdam, She revealed Herself in the same position surrounded by the same symbols, but this time the symbols opened up and became significant realities. The nations of the world were revealed on the globe and the clouds swept away to show a flock of sheep which represents all the peoples of the world destined for the one true fold of the one shepherd. The rays of light streaming from the hands of Our Blessed Lady are now shown to be three rays which are: Grace — coming from the Father; Redemption — coming from the Son; and Peace which *will* come from the Holy Spirit.

The times in which we live are the times in which all peoples of the world must be formed in universal unity; first all Christians, and then all the peoples of the earth with a view to the Universal Kingship of Christ and the outpouring of the Holy Spirit.

Beyond the Millennium

> *The times have arrived. The Holy Spirit must come upon the earth. The Holy Spirit must again come down and this time it will be upon all peoples. For it is now **and only now** that the Holy Spirit will come upon the earth.*

Our Lady comes to announce the Holy Spirit and She comes to prepare the way for this. When He comes, when He returns, will there yet be faith upon earth? Scripture tells us that the earth will be enveloped in the Darkness of the Mystery of Iniquity; in the Liturgy of the Epiphany it says "Darkness will cover the earth and a mist the peoples."

The Mystery of Iniquity has already begun and is by no means over, but the Blessed Virgin Mary announces the great light of the great dawn of the Epiphany and She is the column of cloud in the desert of the world in which we live. She was sent that She might lead all peoples to the Glory of the Epiphany.

*I come in order to be the Lady of all Peoples, not of one people in particular, but of **All Peoples**. I desire to come among the peoples who are kept far from my Son for these things concern the entire world.*

During the first phase of Revelation only the Father made Himself known to men, to his people Israel. In the second phase, the Son came "For the salvation of a great number" according to the Word in St. Luke's Gospel. And now on the threshold of the third and final phase, the Holy Spirit is going to come to enkindle the *whole* world.

And Our Blessed Lady who in the beginning was the Immaculate Conception and who once was Mary, now returns under a new title *"THE LADY OF ALL PEOPLES"* and She does so to bring about unity of all nations to make them one with the people of God in one Universal Church.

Beyond the Millennium

God Sent Mary for Unity

Christians will have to unite throughout the entire world. I appeal again to all peoples; it is already late — unite.

It is She alone, Mary the Mother of the Church, who is to form and to bring about this unity, this great body of the new Church.

The Lord and Master wishes to bring spiritual unity to the peoples of this world. It is for this that He sends Mary — and He sends her as the Lady of All Peoples.

During the Second Vatican Council, Pope Paul VI commended to the entire assembly that Mary be recognized and proclaimed as the Mother of the Church, so it is right that She be seen as the leader in this plan of Divine Providence, to bring unity to the world.

At Amsterdam, She warned of the great peril which would befall the Church because of false doctrine and heresy. Already in the pontificate of Pope Paul VI an insiduous attack was being launched casting doubt upon the Real Presence in the Eucharist and undermining the very foundations of the Catholic Church. Our Blessed Lady asked that Rome be made aware of this error which She said would have its origin in the Netherlands.

Let the clergy be warned, let them be put on their guard against false doctrines, particularly in what concerns the Eucharist. The Lord Jesus Christ has left you the great mystery, the great miracle of each day, of each hour, of each minute; He has given Himself. No, you peoples of the world, not an idea, no — understand what He proclaimed — not an idea, but Himself under the form of a small piece of bread and under the form of wine.

The Eucharist holds a prominent place in the messages of the Lady of All Peoples and it is through the Eucharist that the world can be saved in this time of darkness. Moreover, Our

Beyond the Millennium

Lady confirms that this is why she chose Amsterdam, *"the city of the miracle"* to come to proclaim Her message. It was at Amsterdam that the great prophecy outlined in Genesis, and the forms under which it will enter history, and the design of God into the actions of men, became explicit.

It is significant that She reveals herself with Her feet firmly placed on Germany and Holland, as if to stress that it is from these countries in particular that the internal schism in the Church over the Eucharist will come. But in the end, Her message is one of triumph, to look beyond the darkness to the light, to the light of the Epiphany.

> *When the time of the Lord Jesus Christ will arrive, you will see that the false prophets, wars, dissensions and disputes will disappear. This time is going to come and there will be Peace, true Peace. Peoples, this true Peace is the Kingdom of God and it is closer than ever. Let these words be clearly understood.*

It is written in St. Matthew's Gospel, "The Good News of the Kingdom will be proclaimed throughout the whole world as a witness to *ALL PEOPLES*. And then the end will come." (Mt. 24-14)

Church Notification

Diocese of Haarlem

Notification
for the Catholic faithful of the diocese of Haarlem

We, the Bishop and Auxiliary Bishop of Haarlem have, for a long time and in increasing numbers, received requests both from home and abroad. These requests are for us to provide clarification regarding the status of the apparitions of Mary as "THE LADY OF ALL PEOPLES (NATIONS)" in Amsterdam, during the years 1945-1959.

After ample consideration and consultation of official authorities, we have decided to adopt the following policy in order to provide the required pastoral clarity:

Beyond the Millennium

Distinction must be made between the apparitions/messages on the one hand and the Marian title "The Lady of All Peoples (Nations)" on the other hand.

At the moment the Church cannot make a pronouncement about the supernatural character of the apparitions and the content of the messages. One is free to make a personal judgment according to his or her own conscience.

The prayer "Lord Jesus Christ..." which includes the title "The Lady of All Peoples (Nations)" has since 1951 enjoyed Church approval by Msgr. Huibers, who was Bishop of Haarlem at the time. It is our judgment that there is no objection against the public veneration of the Blessed Virgin Mary under this title.

In an age where races, peoples and cultures are more dependent on each other than ever before — nowhere more so than in Amsterdam — we have confidence in saying that it is exactly this title which throws a clear light on our Lady's Universal Motherhood and her unique role as "woman" in God's plan of Salvation.

Haarlem, 31st of May 1996, on the Feast of The Visitation of Mary.

+Hendrik Bomers +Joseph Punt
Bishop of Haarlem Auxiliary

Beyond the Millennium

Introduction

The Age of Mary - Marian history and the time of Divine Mercy, run parallel but in reality are but one and the same grace given us in preparation for the time of Peace, the Age of the Holy Spirit in the Eucharistic Reign of Jesus, when there will be one flock, one Church, and one shepherd.

Our Blessed Lady comes to lead humanity towards the Age of Her Divine Spouse, the One True Spirit. By the grace of God Her visible presence is manifested more and more in every country of the world, and Her voice is heard more clearly than ever before, as Jesus continues to pour out the love of His Divine Heart and His mercy on an ungrateful humanity.

Beyond the Millennium

From the Word of the Holy Spirit through the Evangelists, St. Paul, the saints, especially those of modern times, and through seers and privileged souls, to whom the charism has been given to prophesy *some* aspects of future events, it is possible, in part, to place into perspective some of the significant elements of God's plan for the fulfillment of His promise for a time of true Peace.

It's not surprising however, and understandable perhaps in a way, that with the plethora of messages, signs and prophecies which proliferate at this time, some of them true, many sadly, deviated, and because of the confusion and darkness worldwide, there is a tendency to set a timetable, humanly speaking, for God to exercise His Will.

Informants on all sides put forward how and when events will unfold, conditional or otherwise, and in this rush to explain everything, the fulfillment of how Our Lord's Agony, Passion, Crucifixion and Resurrection will be lived out in the Church, and in the whole world, becomes confined to a very short time frame, without room for ordered development or to allow the power of God to act freely in response to repentance and reparation.

In looking at the end of our times, the fifth era of Christianity, known as the Age of Purgation and Suffering, and in anticipation of the reign of the Spirit of Peace, the period of preparation for the End of Time and the Final Judgement, we can see a definite pattern in Mary's role, and Her responsibility to bring about this Reign of the Holy Spirit, dating back to that breathtaking moment in 1531 when She left Her true image on Blessed Juan Diego's cloak at Tepeyac and in so doing, laid down Her visible challenge to Satan, that here was the One who was going to crush his head with Her heel.

Her triumph, Her victory, will only be truly manifested, first, when the last Dogma in Marian history will have been proclaimed by Pope John Paul II, the Pontiff charged by God to carry this out, and second, when She is crowned the Lady of all Peoples (All Nations), and then finally, when the Two Hearts of Jesus and Mary are united with all the hearts and souls in the Mystical Body. Sadly, very many

Christians today still persist in a deafness, refusing to listen to, or obey, the Word of Christ or accept His invitation seeking to unite them in a one single Church founded by the innocent lamb who died for men. Why do so many separated Christians want to remain apart from the one Catholic Church, when if rejoined to the true vine they would be sustained by the sacraments and unity? Instead, they deprive themselves of so much good because of their obstinacy in separation.

Although other Churches and Christian bodies do not lack many upright of heart, it is sad to see how they mutilate and sterilize this virtue by wanting to remain severed from the trunk of Roman Catholicism, whose roots are bedded in the Apostles and the early Christians in the catacombs, and whose top now touches the heavens from Rome; for the One, Holy, Apostolic, Roman Catholic Church was not created by proud patriarchs, or by any one man, even if a king, or by an ex-Communicate already marked with the sign of hell, or by schismatics, but by God made Man, the Eternal Triune Holy King.

Too many Christians though, who knowing Christ as Orthodox, Anglicans, Lutherans, Methodists, Calvinists and Evangelicals, trample on even the proof of Love which Christ has given for their salvation; His humiliations. They prefer to be spiritually dead, when they could be alive, because of their obstinate will to remain apart.

They *try* to feel God and bring God to be felt, even speaking the language of God and His saints, so as to persuade themselves that they belong to Him and are saved by Him.

But the sadness of separation is on them and in them. They are in effect the false rich, the false well-fed, desiring to be nourished but remaining hungry and very, very poor, for the great treasures of Roman Catholicism, the infinite treasures of Christ, the Head of His Church, are closed to them.

Jesus is the Bread of Heaven, the intact Bread which experiences no manipulation by man - Jesus, intact, holy and gentle, descended from Heaven to earth. The pain of separation from the Father and Spirit marked the entry of the Light into the midst of darkness. For thirty-three years, at an increasing pace, the Life of Christ was nothing but a succession of humiliations, no one more annihilated than He, more misunderstood by ignorant well-meaning friends and by resentful enemies. *"He who never committed sin or uttered deceitful words, who when cursed did not curse, when ill-treated did not threaten, and placed Himself in the hands of those judging Him unjustly, bore our sins Himself, in His Body on the Cross."* (1 Peter 2:22-24)

His Word fills the heavens created by Him and they bear witness to Him, just as everything created bears witness to His providential Power and events *confirm* prophecies, so there's no doubt that the Eternal Word is King, Savior, Redeemer and therefore the *only* Shepherd.

"...And He has ordered us to proclaim this to His people and to tell them that God has appointed Him to judge everyone, alive or dead. It is to Him that all the prophets bear this witness." (Acts 10:42-43.)

St. Paul says, *"Prophecies have an essential purpose to fulfill, but can tend to influ-*

*ence emotional people to **unbalanced** ideas."* Prophecies exist for our spiritual guidance **not** to gratify our curiosity. Knowledge implies responsibility.

Revelation

Before the complete purification of *our* times, can and will take place, in the Justice of God the Father, like the purification of the Jews, His chosen people, prior to their entry into the Promised Land, first the Age of Mary must come to a close allowing the Holy Spirit time and freedom to renew all things in Christ.

A moment will come, as Our Lady has revealed through private revelation, when She will "withdraw," when Her apparitions will cease and Her message will be complete, a moment when, *if* Our Lord's outpouring of Divine Mercy will have been finally rejected, when it will have become inert because of closed hearts, the Justice of God the Father must prevail and the Holy Spirit will come to scorch the world and humanity in the fire of His love of purification.

But, before this can happen, we shall be privileged to witness the crowning glory of the Age of Mary with the proclamation and recognition of Her role in salvation - Co-Redemptrix, Mediatrix and Advocate, the Lady of All Peoples (Nations).

Through the deceased visionary, Ida Peerdeman in Amsterdam, Our Lady revealed many times that these events would be accomplished in the years '51, '53, '54. Of course, these 'coded' dates do not refer to 1951, 1953, or 1954, nor do they refer to the next century.

3-28-1951

"...Some time ago I showed you the dates '51, '53. Do you know child, what period this is? It is a time almost unprecedented in history - such a falling away from the Faith. You do not know what the future holds. You have no idea of the great danger in which Rome is situated."

12-8-1952

*"The Lady says slowly and distinctly, '... '53, we are on the **eve** of great decisions.'"*

5-10-1953

"... '53 is the year of the Lady of All Peoples (Nations). It is the year in which She must be made known under the title the Lady of All Peoples (Nations.) It is the year in which great world events and worldwide calamities will happen."

10-11-1953

"'... '53 is the year of the Lady of All Nations, the year in which She must be made known under this title amongst All Nations; the year in which great world events will happen.' Again, the Lady with that thoughtful expression says very slowly and distinctly, *'The*

> *year '53 is the year in which the Lady must be brought to the world.'*
>
> *'First, however, let the Church and the Nations invoke Mary under this new title and say the prayer so that moral decline, disasters, and war, may be averted. If they do this, the peoples of Europe will be at peace after '54. See to the Dogma - the crowning of the Mother of The Lord Jesus Christ, Co-Redemptrix, Mediatrix and Advocate. In '54 She must be announced with this new title to the Nations.'"*

From other messages given to Ida, as well as from these, it seems there would be an acknowledgement in the year '51, a proclamation in '53 and a coronation in '54.

Providentially, the acknowledgment came in 1996 on May 31st when the Bishop of Haarlem gave his formal approval for veneration of the Lady of All Nations, in an official Episcopal letter (see previous section).

From this we might come to understand that 1996 (51 years after the first apparition in

1945) refers to the year '51. However, it is probably more correct to see the years '50, '51, '52, '53 and '54, all of which Our Lady refers to, as directly related to the priesthood of Pope John Paul II (50 years a priest in 1996) and the preparatory years of the Millennium, 1997, 1998, 1999 and the Jubilee year itself, in which case this would be the year '54 talked about by Our Lady. We shall have to wait and see if events prove it, for Our Lady said She would give no signs - the only signs would be when events were fulfilled.

The prophecies and prophetic dreams of St. John Bosco are as extraordinary and as numerous as the *miracles* attributed to him. To this day, over a hundred years after his death, there is still a continuing interest and curiosity in trying to discern the enigma of the different *façades* of the Basilica of Our Lady Help of Christians in Turin, which he designed, and where, with coded symbols and dates he prophesises the precise moment of the total defeat and final downfall of the powerful Freemasonic political machine in that city, and in fact, throughout the world. This enigma is yet to be fully discerned. Never short of witty devices, John Bosco frequently used them to confuse the enemies of the Church and to conceal the heart of his prophetic message.

One dream in particular which he transcribed in full, has special relevance for our time, as it relates specifically to the fulfillment of Our Lord's promise of an Era of Peace; it also confirms this will not be achieved without a fierce spiritual struggle.

January, 1870

On the eve of the Epiphany of the year 1870, all the material objects of my room disappeared and I found myself in the presence of supernatural things. It lasted for a few moments during which time I saw many things. Although the form they took was of a perceptible appearance, it is nevertheless difficult to communicate what I saw through external and tangible signs. What follows will give some idea. Here we have God's word mixed with human words.

1. *The war comes from the South, peace from the North. The laws of France no longer recognize the Creator, but the Creator will make Himself known and on three occasions He will visit France with the rod of His anger. The first time, He will shatter her pride through defeats, devastation, destruction of harvests, animals and people. On the second occasion, Paris will be deprived of a leader and will be prey to disorder.*

    Paris...Paris! Instead of arming yourself with the name of the Lord, you surround yourself with houses of ill repute. These will be destroyed by yourself: your idol, the Pantheon will be burned down... Your enemies will deliver you up to anguish, will expose you to famine, to terror and to the hatred of the nations. But woe to you if you fail to recognize the hand that strikes you! I intend to punish immorality, neglect and contempt of My law!" **says the Lord.**

Beyond the Millennium

> *On the third occasion, you will fall into the hands of foreigners; your enemies will look from afar as your palaces burn, and your dwellings become a heap of ruins soaked in the blood of good people who are no more.*

2. *But behold, a great warrior from the North holding in his right hand a standard on which is written:* **irresistible hand of the Lord.**

   At that moment, the venerable Old Man from Latium comes to meet him, brandishing a flaming torch. Then the standard will unfurl and from the black color that it was it will become as white as snow. In the middle of the standard, written in letters of gold, is the name of the One who can do all things.

   The warrior and his men bow profoundly before the Old Man and shake his hand. Now the voice from Heaven addresses the Pastor of pas-

tors. 'You and your assessors are now in a great reunion, but the enemy of the good is not resting. He is studying and employing every device against you; he will raise up enemies from among My sons. The powers of this world will vomit fire and will stifle the words of the guardians of My law. It will not be. They will work evil, but they will do it against themselves. Hurry, hurry. Though your difficulties remain, at least they will be broken. If you find yourself in difficulty, do not stop, but carry on until the hydra head of error is broken. This blow will cause earth and hell to tremble, but the world will be reassured and the good will rejoice. Keep at your side only two assessors, but wherever you go continue and complete the work entrusted to you. The days pass quickly, your years advance towards the preordained hour, but the great Queen will always be your help and, as in the past, She will always be the Church's great and singular protection.

3. *But you, Italy, land of blessings, who plunged you into desolation? It is not your enemies but your friends. Have I not heard that your sons ask for the bread of faith but find no one to give it to them? What shall I do? I shall strike the pastors and scatter the flock so that those who sit on the chair of Moses seek good pasture and that the docile flock hear and are nourished.*

But My hand will strike the flock and the pastors; famine, plague and war will cause mothers to shed tears over the blood of their sons and their husbands dead in enemy lands.

And you Rome, what will become of you? You have come to forget that the glory of your Sovereign and yours too are on Golgotha. Now is the Sovereign old, crumbling, disarmed and stripped bare; and yet with His word alone, He makes the world to tremble.

Rome! I shall come to you four times! The first time I shall strike the land and its inhabitants; the second time, I shall bring defeat and extermination to your very walls. I shall come a third time to knock down the defenses and the defenders, and at the Father's command, a reign of terror, horror and desolation will set in.

But my good children flee, My law is trampled on; that is why I come for a fourth visit. Woe to you if My law is still an idle word for you! There will be prevarication among the learned as well as among the ignorant. Your blood and the blood of your sons will wash the filth with which you besmirch the Law of your God. War, plague, hunger are the scourges with which human pride and malice will be struck. Where now, you rich ones, are your splendors, your villas and your palaces?

Beyond the Millennium

They have become the garbage of the squares and streets. And you, the priests, why do you not weep between the vestibule and the altar pleading for these chastisements to be suspended? Why do you not take the shield of faith and walk on the roof tops; why do you not go into the houses and along the streets to still inaccessible places to carry the seed of My Word? Do you not know that My Word is the terrible two edged sword that defeats My enemies and breaks the anger of God and of nations?

These events will inevitably take place one after the other. Things follow one after the other too slowly, but the august Queen of Heaven is there. The power of the Lord is in her hands. She scatters her enemies like clouds. She clothes the venerable Old Man in all his former vestments. A violent hurricane is still to come; sin has come to an end and,

before the two full moons of the month of the flowers has passed, *the rainbow of peace will appear over the earth. The great Minister will see the Spouse of his King clothed in festive garments. Over the whole world there will appear a sun as bright as the flames of the Cenacle, such as will never be seen from here until the end of time.*

"A great warrior from the north" refers to the Great French Monarch (to come) Henri de la Croix (Henry of the Cross) who will ascend the throne of France, (the Eldest Daughter of the Church, and he, her Eldest Son) — a throne which is rightly his as he is a descendant of Saint King Louis IX and of the Martyr King Louis XVI executed in the French Revolution. He is now in exile at a secret location. Described in many prophecies through the saints and other victim souls as "the Savior," he will come to lead the world at its greatest moment of darkness and peril and renew all things in Christ.

"The Great Queen" is Our Blessed Lady and "The Old Man from Latium" is the Pope.

In the last paragraph, "The month of flowers" is the month of March — the month of St. Joseph and the Annunciation. In Turin where John Bosco lived, March was always known as "the month of the flowers." The only times *two full* moons occur in that month are in the years 1999 and 2001.

The "enemies" into whose hands France will fall are Muslims who in a particularly bloody and terrible occupation lasting a month or so, will bring about an awful persecution of the Church in much of central and southern France, as well as later in Rome and Naples.

The prophecies concerning the Great Monarch and the grave tribulations which will afflict France and Italy and in particular Paris and Rome, are confirmed in much detail through the extraordinary Breton visionary and stigmatist, Marie-Julie Jahenny who died in 1941 at the age of ninety-one.

Jesus to Marie-Julie Jahenny

My little souls, I Myself am preparing a savior for you, yet unknown to the people of the world. His name is engraved on My Divine Heart. His appearance, when revealed, will be seen as a resplendent gift from Heaven, and those who expect him and who have petitioned for his coming, will not be surprised, since My Grace and Light will make them understand that this earthly flower, the Lily of Salvation, has been chosen by Me, but has been kept hidden in My Divine Heart, for I have not disclosed his name.

This soul will come to renew the world, from My poor kingdom (France); *My servant and king will come from My Divine Heart. He will spread wider devotion to My Heart and to My Cross. He will be a new Louis XVI.* (The Martyr King guillotined in 1793, who died for the Church.)

Beyond the Millennium

*My plans for him and for France are great and it is My Holy Mother who, through him, will deliver My people. He will reign and govern for a **long time**.*

His soul shines with purity and loyalty in Faith and he is the one chosen to restore My Mother's Kingdom to Grace, at present plunged into an abyss of crime, iniquity, and vice. He will be revealed in the midst of a very hard battle (war in Europe), *but it will not last long.*

I alone can save you. France cannot be saved by men. I alone will give her her last crown which she will keep until the beginning of the Last Judgement. The king is a lily, (the Fleur de Lis is the emblem of the true French Monarchy), *a hero, whom the world is not yet aware of, but his reign will endure until the end of time, in all the brilliance of his beauty and glory.*

This savior will be needed to rebuild a devastated world, a world which will be much destroyed in many, many places, to rebuild the ruins, and to crush the power of Satan and his empire (false religions).

As for the savior I desire, some will offer themselves as pretenders to the throne but there remain great battles, severe obstacles and hardships. Two false pretenders in succession will ascend the throne at a time of severe crisis for France. They will be removed by lightning from Heaven (St. Michael will remove them). *The reign of My Divine Heart will be unveiled in Heaven from where My Glory will shine down to protect My chosen savior and his **small** elect group.*

My little souls, the savior of My Choice, following the Great Blow (The Chastisement), *during which the whole earth will be strewn with bodies struck down by My Justice, will cross Europe accompanied by My Elect, My Servants and their Spouses. He will march towards his throne which I will have purified with Grace. After a battle* (a spiritual one — no bloodshed) *France will become beautiful again, but many, many will be missing; only My Faithful people will be preserved for this Great Glory.*

Our Blessed Lady to Marie-Julie Jahenny

The king will come at a time of terrible upheavals for the world and for France, which has lost its honor, greatness, beauty and nobility. It is then that a savior unknown as yet to the earth, but who some may have guessed at but not known, will come as a gift from Heaven, as a gift of the Sacred Heart and My Immaculate Heart, the Heart of your Mother.

He will be announced on a day when there will be very little light, under a thick and black sky. The darkness is a sign which will announce the great march of Divine Justice (the approaching Three Days of Darkness).

My children, his place is in the Heart of My Son and it is from there he will come purified and sanctified to start his great work of restoring the world to God which will give great joy to those who are consecrated to Me and who are loved by Me.

My Son will give His servant a clean crown for France, a crown without stain, a crown which will last until the end. (Until the reign of the anti-Christ and the Final Judgement.)

When the earth will have been cleansed from its crimes and from the vices which poison her, I tell you that days of good will return. This savior chosen by Us, unknown to Our children until now, is a beautiful soul, a special flower of purity and virtue. He is adorned with spiritual nobility. The Grace of Heaven will be with him. My beloved children, it is during the third crisis that he will come. With his coronation all evil will cease. He is a descendant of Saint King Louis (Louis IX).

Beyond the Millennium

Marie-Julie Jahenny was born into a peasant family in 1850 in the village of Coyault, not far from Blain, but lived most of her life in the hamlet of La Fraudais about 2$^1/_2$ miles away.

As a child she was very devout but did not receive any mystical experiences until she was over twenty. Her parents were very poor, so instead of being able to go to school, she had to work. She did, however, have six months of schooling on the catechism when she learned to read, but she never did learn to write.

At age twenty-three she fell seriously ill and was given the Last Rites. Shortly after, she suddenly sat up in bed, her eyes wide open, gazing motionless in front of her, then fell back as if dead. When she recovered, she said that Our Blessed Lady had appeared to her. A few weeks later She appeared again, and this time asked Marie-Julie if she would accept the five wounds of Jesus and would she also suffer all her life for the conversion of sinners. *"Yes, with all my heart, if this is what Jesus wishes and if He finds me worthy of it"* Marie-Julie replied. *"My dear child, this will be your mission"* Our Lady told her.

Six days later on Friday, March 21st, she received the wounds, and some months on, also Christ's crown of thorns and the holy wound of His shoulder. For sixty-eight years she never ceased to suffer the Passion of Our Lord. Each Tuesday and Thursday, in ecstasy, she experienced apparitions not only of Jesus and His Mother, but of many of the saints and angels. Like many seers privileged to receive prophecy of future events, and a spiritual understanding of them, she was given a "Divine Sun" (a flame of the Holy Spirit) to contemplate, in which events were brought to her knowledge. (Others to whom this gift was given were St. Thomas Aquinas, St. Margaret Mary, and Anna Maria Taigi.)

In all, Marie-Julie experienced more than three thousand apparitions.

In addition to the physical torture of Christ's Passion, she suffered the moral anguish of having been abandoned and judged, not by her family who remained steadfast and supportive, but by her own people and the local Church hierarchy, as well as being betrayed by malicious gossip-mongers who bitterly calumniated her in her virtue of purity. She was condemned by two successive parish priests, and deprived of the sacraments for eleven years. Her spiritual director was taken from her, and Bishop Fournier who was favorably disposed, died and was replaced by a bishop who did not believe, and at first ignored strict orders from Pope Leo XIII to give her the sacraments again. A campaign and conspiracy of lies was directed at her with the active participation of many of the clergy.

Eventually, after Fr. Vanutelli, a Dominican and cousin of the Cardinal of the same name, and other influential priests in the Vatican had worked tirelessly for the truth to be known at the Holy Office, Pope Leo again gave direct orders to the French Bishop for the sacraments to be restored to her.

In 1874 Marie-Julie was struck with a sudden and inexplicable deafness which lasted for ten years, although she could hear the priest in Latin, and her own family, as well as the sound of bells and the birds singing.

From 1875 to 1881 she took no food at all, and her bowel and bladder stopped functioning. In 1881 she was struck with paralysis of the left side and was confined night and day to an armchair. This lasted four years. She was also totally blind for this period.

Her father died in 1892, her sister in 1900, her mother in 1908 and her brother in 1922. From then on she lived alone in her little cottage.

Most of the prophecies were made between 1873 and 1878, but throughout her life she was the recipient of Divine Inspiration.

In her long life she lived to see France devastated by three wars, the Franco-Prussian War of 1870/71, the First World War, which Our Lord warned her in 1914 was imminent, and the Second World War about which Jesus spoke to her in 1918 when the Armistice was signed concluding the First War.

*"If My people do not come back to Me, if they do not acknowledge Me as their Sovereign Lord, I shall enkindle My Justice again. There will be few conversions but **not** of those who should be first to confess their unfaithfulness*

*and their contempt for My Divine Person. If these people do **not** acknowledge Me, My Justice will prevail again; I am not satisfied with so little thanksgiving."*

War broke out again in 1939. In November of that year, Marie-Julie warned it would be a long one and that is would finish badly.

In 1937 she had received a private and unexpected visit from one of the most influential men in the Vatican. Cardinal Pacelli, (Pius XI's Cardinal Secretary of State) later, Pope Pius XII, had come to France as papal Legate to open and bless the new Basilica at Lisieux. He took advantage of that trip to visit Marie-Julie secretly and have a long conversation with her. (He was already well-acquatinted with the papers describing Marie-Julie's ecstasies - which had been entrusted to the Holy Office by Monsignor Le Fer de la Motte, Bishop of Nantes, 1914-1935, who not only often visited La Fraudais but was a firm supporter of the seer, and who recognized the vital importance of her apostolate for the Church and the world.) In 1956 on the occasion of the 400th anniversary of St. Joan of Arc's death, Pius XII, in the course of his address by radio, said this - *"It is not a rare thing that at the most critical moments, the Lord sends the supernatural inspiration which, like a breath of wind that disperses the clouds and lets the star be seen which will guide the navigator to his port of destination, makes of a soul the salvation of people."* Although not mentioning her by name, the Holy Father had in mind with these words, Marie-Julie, the seer of La Fraudais. The papers on her unique mission are to this day kept in safekeeping in the Vatican, secure from the grasp of the Freemasonic enemies of the church who would surely destroy them if they could get hold of them.

In general, the prophecies through Marie-Julie bear on a wide range of events concerning events during her own lifetime, and those foreseen in the struggle ahead to renew all things in Christ.

> *1. The Church: New liturgy, worldwide apostasy, passivity of bishops, innovative priests, scandals and sacri-*

> *leges in churches, sacrilegious communions, persecution and devastation of the Church as an organization.*

2. *A grave warning for the whole of humanity.*

3. *The work of Freemasonry through governments, parliaments, republics and democracies.*

4. *The victory of Marxist/Communism.*

5. *Wars and revolution worldwide.*

6. *The extent of the death toll.*

7. *Tribulations in France and in Italy, in Paris and in Rome in particular.*

8. *An Act of God to destroy the enemies of the Church, the ascendancy of a great Christian King, chosen by God to free the rightful Pope, to re-*

store order and to have France and the world reconsecrated to the Sacred Heart.

Through Marie-Julie, as through other seers, we are made aware of a grave warning which Divine Mercy will extend to the whole world.

One way of describing this warning is as a mini-judgment, but it will be much more like each soul seeing its own personal darkness as compared to the pure Light of God. Every soul, every human-being, without exception, will see its sins and how much Almighty God is offended by them each day. This is necessary because humanity no longer realizes the extent to which God is offended.

Following the illumination of the soul in this way, those who repent, will be given an overwhelming hunger for the Light of Christ.

Modern trends, the standards of the world as we know them in our generation, and sadly, the teaching of the Catholic Church, (in some cases,) which tends to the idea that sin is irrelevant — only a small offense and that God will not be offended by it — gives a false indication of the Justice of God, for whilst He is perfectly merciful to those who repent, He is also perfectly just to those who do not.

God will allow the pain and suffering of this Judgement, for love through suffering is His way of Redemption.

This great event *will* take place and everyone should prepare to meet God, for we shall all see ourselves at that moment, as He sees us.

There is much speculation today about the timing of Our Lord's intervention to illuminate the soul in this unprecedented way — especially since the early 1960's when visionaries at Garabandal in northern Spain confirmed for our generation the certainty of the forthcoming event, but without revealing the date or the year.

Our Divine Lord did, however, reveal to Marie-Julie the season in which the warning would happen, placing it in the month of March.

June 15th 1882

"I forewarn you, a day will come when in the early hours of the morning there

*will be little light from the sun, or from the stars; it will be in the early month of the year. There will be insufficient light for people to leave their houses. It will **not** be in mid-summer, not during the longest days, nor during the shortest ones. It will not be at the end of the year, not in December but rather when the spring wheat will not quite have reached its third notch of growth. (March.) It will be a day of continuous thunder and lightning and terrible upheavals in the atmosphere. The sun will be almost completely darkened. This will start mid-day (in France) lasting 'till 4:00 p.m. It will signal the commencement of the Chastisement of the earth."*

It was also revealed that a solar prodigy and a Cross visible in the sky all over the world will be linked to the Warning. Further, it will be associated with the letter 'A' — it will not fall on a Feastday of Our Lady.

Coincidentally, the announcement of such a Warning was not revealed only to Marie-Julie and to the visionaries at Garabandal, but in fact, many years earlier, in 1830, to St. Catherine Laboure in the convent in the Rue du Bac, where Our Blessed Lady revealed the secret of the date. The day was also announced to Sr. St. Peter of Tours at about the same time and noted in five "Little Scrolls" of this seer of the Holy Face of Jesus. The scroll will remain concealed until the day when a person named by God will lay his (or her) predestined hand on what the world has not yet been permitted to see. (The writings of Sister St. Peter were put in a secret place in Tours by order of Bishop Morlot in August 1850.)

Our Lord reveals, therefore, to Marie-Julie that the Warning will take place in the month of March, but it is through the Spanish visionary, Amparo Cuevas, in El Escorial in 1982 that we know the circumstances which will precipitate the phenomena.

This is the message given to Amparo at "El Escorial," during an ecstasy in 1982.

"Soon a Warning will be given which will affect all people everywhere.

> *"Each and every person will see the Warning and will understand its meaning. When the Warning comes there will be those who will be so terrified that they will die from sheer fright."*

Her advice is that if you can, you should spend the night in prayer in front of the Blessed Sacrament in church, or in your home with the doors firmly closed. When the Warning comes many will be so frightened by its effects that they will die.

> *"A star, the Asteroid Eros, will illuminate the earth causing it to appear to be surrounded by flames during a period of some twenty minutes, an event which will spread panic everywhere. All those who believe in God and the Holy Virgin will remain in a kind of ecstasy during this period. This will occur in the near future.*
>
> *"When Eros lights up the earth making it appear that the whole world is in flames, many people will wish to die at*

that moment in that shower of fire, which will strike fear in everyone, a fear which will in fact cause the death of many people; those who are just and who believe, will not suffer."

Evidently, NASA launched a space probe February 1996 to find out more about this asteroid, the details of which are known to them.

Amparo was given her message in 1982. The asteroid is due into the earth's orbit in 1999.

The effect of an asteroid passing through the earth's magnetic field, apart from the tremendous climatic upheaval this would cause, would be to bring about a reversal of human consciousness, away from self towards God, enabling us to recognize His all powerful infinite existence as creator of all things outside of Himself.

This wonderful manifestation of His Mercy will be followed *very* soon after by an even greater miracle of His appearance in Garabandal in all His Resurrected Glory, to reveal to the world His Divinity and Sacred

Humanity — God-made-Man, Risen from the Dead, as He said He would.

If these loving and prodigious gifts of Grace are finally rejected, Our Gentle Lord will withdraw to allow the Justice of God the Father to purify the whole of humanity. This Purification will take place in a series of unconditional tribulations in three phases, lasting approximately $3^1/_2$ years — see Johns Bosco's dream as it refers to France and Italy.

Just as he and Ida Peerdeman were shown coded dates to protect the exact timing of future events, so too Marie-Julie was frequently drawn to the years '80, '82, '83, during which these tribulations would take place and when the Chastisement would be complete. Evidently these years do not refer to 1880-1883 nor 2080-2083. Their true identity as yet has not been disclosed and remain hidden except to a few privileged souls.

There are, however, many prophecies by Marie-Julie directly concerning the present Pope, John Paul II, the last *authentically* elected Pope of our times, so perhaps it is interesting to note he will be eighty in the year 2000, the Millennium.

Beyond the Millennium

Throughout the prophecies of Marie-Julie, it is clear that when "The Deluge" — the Purification will come, it will have a depth that no intelligence can begin to estimate or imagine: after all, as Our Lady reminds us, nothing like this will have ever been experienced before; but not all will perish.

"The earth" Our Lady tell us *"will become an abyss, a gaping hole in which both the just and sinner, the priests and lay people will perish.* (Confirmed by Her message given to Sr. Agnes Sasagawa at Akita, 1973.) But a small number of privileged souls will be preserved to *"sing the Hymn of Peace"* a "Te Deum" when the anointed saviour, the king, will ascend the throne prepared by Jesus Himself. Our Lord will preserve also some unbelievers, among them a number of Jews, so that they can see and *acknowledge* the triumph of the Immaculate Heart of His Holy Mother so much maligned by Her own race throughout history.

The 3 $\frac{1}{2}$ year period of tribulation will be a terrible one for the Church, as it lives out the crucifixion and death of Our Lord. We presently see Her in Her Agony in the Garden. Out of this time of trial and condemnation, only a small remnant will remain faithful to the Holy Father and to the Truth of Christ.

"Furthermore, all the leaders of Judah, the priests and the people too, added infidelity to infidelity, copying all the shameful practices of the nations, and defiling the Temple of God which He Himself consecrated in Jerusalem. The God of their ancestors continuously sent them word through His messengers because He felt sorry for His people and His dwelling, but they ridiculed the messengers of God, they despised His words, they laughed at His prophets, until God's anger with His people became so fierce, there was no further remedy." (2 Chronicles 36:14-16.)

Will He find anyone of Faith when He comes? Praise God, Our Lady is gathering Her "chicks" under the mantle of Her wing, to be ready for the Great Day, the coming of Our Lord, in His Euchristic Reign.

Beyond the Millennium

Heaven, Divine Providence, establishes a link between the *longevity* of the French "savior" and the Coming of the Reign of the anti-Christ and the Final Judgement. *"He will be the Last One and Forever."* For afterward, everything will be finished. Christ intends to give to France her last crown, (her last Monarch) and she will keep it until the beginning of the Judgement. This Great King will bring Peace, True Peace, the Peace of the Holy Spirit which will last until France at last enters her grave, at the eve of the end of the world. His reign, we are told will last some thirty-five to forty years, the longest time possible before the anti-Christ (confirmed by the Blessed Virgin Mary at La Salette when she told Melanie Calvat that the Era of Peace would be of approximately thirty to thirty-five years.) However, only God knows the time and the hour of Judgement. *"Be prepared"* Jesus says *"for I will come like a thief in the night."*